Inspirational Poems
"From the Heart and Soul"

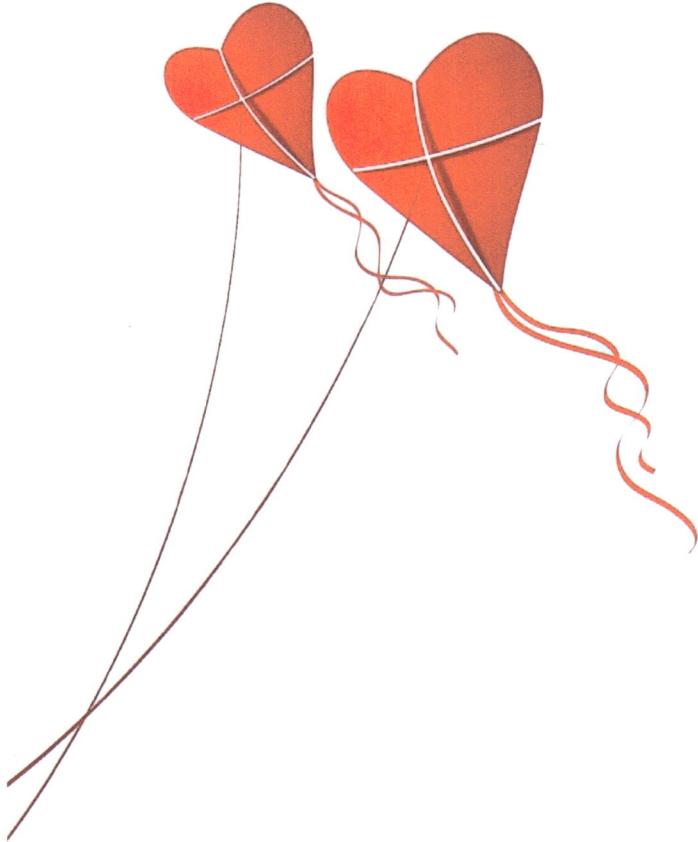

Karen J. Nolan

A special thank you to MaryLou for designing the cover to my poem book.

Photography by John Zogaria
www.BetweenPoses.com

Book Publishing, Book Design, Illustrations, Marketing by
DM BOOKPRO
http://BookPublishing Easy.com

Dedication

I am dedicating this poem book
to my Forever Friend who has
inspired me to write these
Love poems from my Heart

Introduction

My name is Karen Nolan and I am a 3 ½ year Cancer Survivor. I am so thankful and grateful for a second chance in life. Each and every day is a Blessing.

I have been very blessed after all my Cancer Treatments to have the astonishing gift given to me by God to become an author. This poem book is my fifth book so for. I have a feeling that there will be another one within a year. My next book could be a Love Story.

In this book I have written fifty-five poems from the Heart and one poem is from my Soul.

I hope these poems will Inspired you and bring you Love, Peace and Joy to your Hearts like it did mine.

ENJOY!

Acknowledgments

To God who helped me through both of my Journey's.
Also for bringing Shauna my Guardian Angel into
My life.

To my Forever Friend who inspired me
to write these poems.

To my Sister Chris and my Grandson Erick for
supporting me in my new journey of seeking
a Divorce.

To all my caretakers and support system who helped me
to get where I am now in my life.

Special thanks to all my doctors at Rochester Regional
Health and the Lipson Cancer Center,
who took good care of me.

Dr. Medeiros, my Surgeon, Dr. Jamshed,
my Oncologist, And Dr. Atanas, my Radiologist.

Poems from the Heart

Love

Table of Contents

A Soul Mate

A Soul mate is someone
Who knows your thoughts
And what you are caring about

There is Love in both your Hearts
There is never a doubt
When you find your true Soul mate
Ask them to go on a date

Then hope he kisses you not a
Moment too late
This will seal the deal for
Our new fate

It's Springtime

The winter frost has finally
Gone away
Now spring has sprung today

Birds are singing
Tulips and daffodils are blooming
Sweet smells of the fresh air
And the grass is turning different
Shades of green

It's time for Easter with all
The little girls dressing up in
Their pretty dresses

Chocolate bunnies, marshmallows
Chicks and Jelly beans in all
Our Easter baskets
What a beautiful time of year
So much fun and joy
It's a time to cheer

Valentine's Day

It's the time for Lovers to say I Love You
To each other
Boxes of Chocolates and beautiful Red roses
Are given at this time to your
Sweetheart or your Mother
Picking out a beautiful sentimental card
To give or send to your other

Inside the card you write a Heartfelt
Love poem or what you are thinking
About on this very special day
Then take your Sweetheart out to
Celebrate and give her the long stem
Red roses that were so carefully picked
For her bouquet

Happy Valentine's Day

A Dove in my Tree

This beautiful white dove has been sent
To me from Heaven above to bring magic
To my tree

The winter frost wasn't so kind to you
As far as I can see

This dove made a nest for all to be
You flew so gracefully around my
Head to let me know
That you were sent from God and the
Angels above
Just for me

You did bring magic to my tree and then
You magically disappear
And now you can go and rest

I hope my tree will have magic next year

Tap Dancing

Today is my first day of taking
A tap dance class

Putting on my black leotards
Tap shoes with satin ribbons
That needed to be tied and my tights
Feeling like a big girl because I am Only eight
Going to dance class with my Very best friend
And I can't wait

Hoping I can stay in rhythm with
The beat of the music
This could be very confusing

We will be dancing underneath so Many lights
That will be so shiny bright

Clicking my shoes and hearing the taps
On the bottom of my feet
Is making me so proud
One day when I have learned a complete Dance
I can dance in front of a large crowd

Halloween

Summer had come an end
Fall is here
The air has begun to be a little Chilly
Halloween is very near

It's time for children to dress-up
In their favorite costumes
A Ghost, Disney princess, Fireman
Super-heroes, Witches with a broom or
Maybe a Clown

Gathering their pails and going trick Or treating
Having so much fun underneath
The midnight sun
Running and skipping all around the Town
Hoping for so many sweets like
M an M's, Snickers, Milky Ways
And Reese's Peanut Butter Cups
These candies needed to be found
You need to be so careful not to drop
Your pail on the ground
It might make a huge sound

Pumpkins have been carved out and
Looking pretty scary
All lit up with colored lights
This is very eerie

My Cat "Cupcake"

You were so little when you were born
On that day in July
You were so soft and cuddly
And you touched my heart
I didn't have to ask why

You were so cute and all black
With a circle of white on Your chest
I was impressed
You looked like a Hostess Cupcake
I knew then that would be
Your new name very soon
This would not be a mistake

To my surprise as you got a little older
You turned multicolor
Black, grey and white
What a beautiful sight

Cupcake you will always be in my heart

Season "Spring"

The winter frost has Finally gone away
The radiant sun Is shining so bright
In the sky today

Trees are turning a leafy green
Birds are flying and singing
Making so much magic that I can see
The grass is growing and
Turning different colors
Of shades of greens
So much beauty all around
So much magic is to be seen

Kids playing and riding
Their bikes and playing
Hide and seek

When the day is done the
Sun goes away after a very Long day

Then the stars come out and
Take over where the sun
Left off Cache

Tea Kettle

Your water's in the small porcelain tea pot
On the stove
Steaming and bubbling to the music
That flows
Waiting for it to get very hot
So we can hear the whistle sing
When the boiling stops we
Pour the water into our cups
This is a sure thing

Add a cinnamon tea bag and smell
The delicious spice throughout the house
Add cream and sugar and drink up
Being so quiet as a mouse

Drink this tea under the night light
With all our might

Snow Angels in the Snow

Snow is falling down from the Heavens above
Magic from the Angels creating
A white landscape so we can go out
And play with your Winter gloves
You lay down in the snow spreading
Your arms and feet
Which feels like you are taking a flight
Don't give up the fight

Looking up at the sky watching all the
Little sprinkles of snow flurries
Falling down from the sky
Try to catch one on your lips before
They magically disappear before your eyes

Angels are made
It's time to brush off the snow that's
All over your clothes
Even your nose
Make a snowball and throw it at the one
You Love with your nice warm
Winter gloves

Time to go in now
Tomorrow is another day
To come out and play

Christmas Cookies

It's once again a magical time for Christmas
Time to put up lights everywhere and
Decorate Christmas trees
That will shimmer so shining Bright
Now it's time to think about baking
Christmas cookies for everyone to
Enjoy at this time of the year

Gathering your ingredients and cookie cutters
There's no time to wait
So many we have to make
Cookies cutters come in many different
Size and shapes, What a debate

I don't know which one I should use
There are Santa's, Stars, Bells, Angels
Reindeers and Tree's
Oh my, What will be my excuse!

I guess I will start with a Santa first
Cut them out, place them on a sheet
And bake in the oven until golden brown
This is pretty sweet

Smelling the buttery and sugary aroma
Of the cookies baking throughout the House
This is so breathtaking
When they're done take them out of the oven
Being so careful
They are still piping hot
Be very gentle

When cooled you frost each one with a
Creamy confectionary frosting
Add different colors of sprinkles and
Cinnamon drops

The scrumptious flavor of the first bite
Gives a yummy taste to your mouth and tummy
They are made with a lot of Love
Give some to your Honey

My Cat Mittens

I adopted you a long time ago
From the Humane Society
You were so little, fluffy and cute
I fell in Love with you at first sight
This wasn't a flute

I brought you home and you gave me
Many years of Happiness
Until one day my Grandson Erick
Needed you more

He was stuck in a world that most
Of us do not know about
You were what he asked for

You two fell in Love with each other
You brought much Happiness, Peace and
Joy to your big brother

Thank you Mittens, for
Loving us

My Bird Bath

You sit in the midst of my garden
With the rays of the golden Sunlight
Shining down upon you
Warming up the water in your bowl
For my sparrows to take a bath in
The morning light, this is so true

Surrounding the base of you
There're fragrant columbine
Flowers that the goldfinch
Do enjoy perching their wings
Upon your petals

Cardinals and blue jays land upon you
Each and every day
Take a sip of water and
Then fly away

My White Tail Deer when they
Pass through my yard will stop
To take a drink
Quick as wink

Oh, Birdbath you bring so much
Happiness for all my animals each
And every day

Chipmunk

You went away for the
Winter months to hibernate
From the winter's storm

Today spring has sprung
And I see you have
Finally come out to play
Now that it's warm

There are now two of you
Hustling and bustling around my
Plants and trees

You are so cute and small in
Your striped coat and big bushy tail
That I can see

You scamper around gathering food
From the ground in your little pudgy cheeks
Which could take many weeks

You dig holes to hide your food
Or place them in your nest

Now you can go and rest

Then one day when you need a treat
You know where to seek
You are surely very blessed

A Cup of Hot Chocolate

It's a cold winter day
Waking up to the morning light
Smelling sweet smells of
Chocolaty brew steaming
From the kitchen above
There's one for me and you
What a delight

Sipping the cocoa its warmth
Will warm your heart
What enjoyment drinking
This cup of cocoa with lots
Of marshmallows on top

Add a peppermint stick and
See what magic it brings to you
This will not be a mistake

I might have to add extra
Cream to you because you
Are really very hot

Snowflakes

You fall upon us on a Wintery day
Angels from Heaven sent you Our way

You are little snowflakes
That come to us in many
Shapes on these cold and breezy days

Each and every one of you look like
Jewels that sparkle and twinkle
From an Angel's crown
When you are falling down

You fall on the ground and you
Become a white fluffy
Landscape for all of us to enjoy

Kids get their sleds out and
Slide down big hills and
Make snow balls and throw them
At the ones they Love
Oh boy
What a joy

Stars in the Sky

You are way up in the galaxy so high
You are like shining diamonds in the sky

We wish upon you each and every night
Star Light, Star Bright hope all
My wishes will come true
In the morning light

You have a partner with you every night
Your friend the moon is there
To help you with all his might

You sparkle and twinkle all through the night
What a beautiful site

I would Love to be able
To grab one of your stars
And hold it so very tight

May all my wishes come true tonight

My Mom

Since I was very little I
Always looked up to you
Everything that I know
Today is from you

I remember one day when I was only Three
I stood on a stool so I
Could help wipe the dishes that night
In my pretty dress of Blue

Being so careful not to drop
A dish on my toe
This would be a big no

You made all my dancing
Costumes all by hand
Layers and layers of so many
Colors and rhinestones
That were so shiny bright

Now I can go dance in my
Gorgeous costume that you
Made just for me

Under all the beautiful lights

You made me what I am today, kind
Independent, caring and loving
This is what it should be

As I got older when I needed help
You were always there to support me

You were so strong, amazing and
Fine
I know that you would agree

Mom you are always in my heart

A Rainbow

You are magic in the sky
You appear to us on rainy days
Your beautiful arch of colors
Is so amazing to our eyes
Your colors are red, orange
Yellow, green, blue, indigo and violet
You are so broad and wide, Oh my

We wish upon you and hope
Our wishes will come true
Each and every night

You only stay for a little while
Then you magically
Disappear

Then we have to wait for another
Misty or rainy day
Once again for you to appear
Then we can all cheer
Which could bring a tear

A Bowl of Soup

You are in a pan upon the stove
Steaming and bubbling over
Because you are so very hot
It being a surprise what kind you will be
When you cool down I will
Take a little peak and see

I see that you are buttery and Creamy
And I can't wait until I get to taste
With my tongue how dreamy
You will be

You are in my bowl now and to my
Excitement you are many favorite kind
Potato soup with lots of little pieces
Of white potatoes
Which are cut up so very fine

Yummy, yummy to my tummy
This is the best dinner
This is a winner

Elephants

The elephants Jenny and Lilac
From the Seneca Park Zoo
When they talk they
Hum to you

They are tall and strong and
Peaceful and gentle
They are very proud to be
Just what you see

They come from Africa
Which is very far
Their skin is very rough
And tight
They have tusks of Ivory
So pure and white
They carry themselves with
A lot of pride
They are so big and wide
Oh my

Alphabet Blocks

I remember these blocks so very well
With letters of the alphabet and numbers
Outlines in different colors like
Yellow, red, green and blue
This is so true

With my little hands I constructed a tower
Block by block and
When it was stacked too high
They would surely come
Tumbling down
I watched in amazement as
They fell on to the ground
It's a good thing I had a lot of patience

I was intrigued by the pictures on each
Of these blocks
Someone told me what each picture
Could stand for because I was
Only a little girl

I held a block in my hands and was told
To me that

A stands for apple
B for ball
C for cat and
D for dog

As I listened I could see that on every block the
Picture is exactly what it represents to be

When done playing with my blocks
I would tuck them away in my
Little pink box
I will take them out again on
Another day
So I can play

A Christmas Gift

What I wanted more than
Anything as a gift for Christmas
In 1954 was a cute little dolly
Because I was only eight

In front of my eyes when
Opening my gift was the
Most beautiful doll
That I could ever imagine

Her face glowed with glitter
Her pudge cheeks were
So red and rosy
She had eyes of blue
That just sparkled and twinkled
She had a beautiful smile and
Dark brown hair that was in style

Her name was Karen
Made by the Block Doll Company
In the 1950's
Oh how I will always remember

She had buttons on her tummy and back
When pushed she would nod her head
To answer your questions
Tummy button was a yes nod
Back button was a no nod
She was also called a yes or
No doll
And I loved her so

She brought me many years
Of Happiness and Joy
Throughout my childhood years

I think of those days and it
Brings me to tears

Memories of her will always
Linger in my heart

Miracles

Gods sends us Miracles
From Heaven above for me and you
All you have to do is Believe
And they will come true

They are precious gifts from
Angels and God as our Master
There are messages of Courage to
Those with Faith
Hope to those who Dream
And Love to those who accept

They are send to me and you
With much Love from above
This is the astonishing truth

Happy Birthday

Happy Birthday comes
Once a year
On the same day and
Makes us another year older

I celebrate my Birthday in
A different way
I don't ask for gifts or even
A Chocolate cake
On this day

Life took me down and
I was given a second chance
So for my Birthday
I celebrate Life instead and
Go listen to music and Dance

I am so grateful and thankful
For this second chance
And I have God and the Angels
To thank for that

Happy Birthday !

A Cookie Tray of Love

Valentine's day is very near
Time to bake Valentines cookies
For this special day
For someone who is very dear

Cut them out with a heart
Shaped cookie cutter
Placed on a baking sheet and
Baked until golden brown
Take them out of the oven
Be careful not to drop them
On your feet
Because they are very hot
This wouldn't be very sweet

Now frost each cookie when cooled
With pink confectionary frosting
And add red sprinkles and Cinnamon drops
Now give one to your Honey

These Valentine cookies are made
With a lot's of Love for the one
You are so proud of

Ladybug

Oh lady bug, lady bug
You are so small and cute
With your warm colors of
Red, orange or yellow
With black spots
You are round or an oval-shape
And you hold a special message
For me and you

You are mesmerizing to our eyes
For all to see
You land on our plants and trees

There is a myth about you
That you bring good luck to all
When holding you in our hands
We make a wish upon you and hope
That it will come true

I hope my wishes when wished
Upon you will come true

Daffodils

Winter time is coming to an end
Spring is very near
Snow is now melting away
Then to my amazing surprise
Trumpets of yellow daffodils
Are poking their heads up and
Out of the snow covered ground
God is surely showing then the way
Their color of yellow is so
Breathtaking to our eyes
Not a surprise

Daffodils stand so tall and stiff
In a breeze they flutter their petals
And dance in the wind

There is a special meaning for
The daffodils they give us
Hope to everyone by
Bringing us closer to our Dreams

My Dream is to stay
Cancer free

A Train Set

Underneath the beautiful decorations
Under the Christmas tree
On this day that Jesus was born
There was a gift that was wrapped in paper
Just for me
To my astonishment there was a train set
Inside
What a perfect gift

Now I can't wait until
I can set it up
And enjoy all to be seen
There is a Locomotive Engine
Coal cars and a little Red Caboose too

I can't wait to hear it go
Clicking clack over the
Railroad tracks
Add some houses, buildings
And trees
And lot of people all around
Maybe a bridge or two
A platform for the train to go

Up and over the hills
And all around this little town

This train set brought me so much
Joy and made me smile
I spend many years enjoying this
Special Christmas gift

Memories of it will always
Be in my heart
This is the way it went

A Christmas Card

It's the time of the season to send
A special message to the ones we Love
Who are near or so far away

So many choices that we can make
In picking out a card
This would not be a mistake

There are cards with Santa Claus that
Are dazzling with a lot of glitter, Angels
That are so pure and white on the cover
Reindeer pulling Santa's sleigh
Smiling snowmen on a hill of snow
Little children ice skating on a frozen
Pond or a church with lights
That glow

It's doesn't matter which one you select
Heartfelt meaning is sure to affect
Your loved ones at this Christmas season
You take the card home
Put a stamp on it and mail it out
It gets delivered and it will bring Love

Joy and Happiness to this person
That was on your Christmas list

A Cabin in the Woods

I have always dreamt about
What it would be like to camp in
The woods
Would it be very peaceful and have
A serene feeling being alone with
One you Love

What a beautiful and mesmerizing
Place to be with all the animals
Crisp blue waters of the lake
And the sweet aroma of all the plants
And trees

Taking long walks and holding hands
With all our might
Being so careful not to get stung
By all the bee's tonight

Kicking little pebbles so high
That could touch the sky
Oh my

Sitting by the campfire roasting and

Toasting all those marshmallows
Now it's time to dance with your
Sweetheart under all the stars in the sky
Being so careful not to step on a piece of bark
Kissing your sweetheart in the dark

Thanksgiving

It's the time of the year for Blessings
Time to be grateful and thankful for all
Time to celebrate with family and friends
Enjoying the company and good food
That is served on this special day
Puts you in a good mood

Thanks to the Pilgrims and the
American Indians who discovered
This day and celebrated it with
Corn and a Tom Turkey
Then we pray and say a prayer for
This special Holiday

A Toe Dancer

It's what I wanted to be
When I grew up
Experiencing all the beautiful
Places where I could dance
For the whole world to see

In my pink toe shoes
That took a few years
Of lessons to learn how to
Pivot on my toes
This is the way it goes

I danced with a lot of motion
That makes me feel like I am
Light on my feet with a lot of
Emotion

I never became that dancer that
I wanted to be
Life took a turn on me and I
Had to give up dancing
I do agree

My dreams and wishes of becoming a
Dancer will always linger in my heart
For me

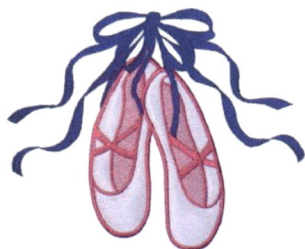

A Cardinal

You perch your magnificent
Red breast on my Rose of
Sharon Tree
Your color of red is so
Mesmerizing for all to see

You sit upon my tree spreading
Your wings and showing off the
Beautiful crest off your red crown
For the whole world to see

As snowflakes fall down from
Heaven above
There sits a cardinal on a frozen
Branch covered with white snow
His red breast is glowing so bright
In the afternoon light
It's so vibrant with beauty of divine
He was sent from God in Heaven above

The cardinal looks for seeds and nuts in
A bird feeder for all to seek
Your treats are found and then you

Fly away to find a mate

Don't be a moment too late
Come back in the spring so we
Can hear your magic when you sing

Beauty of a cardinal will always
Linger on in our eyes to be seen

Wintertime

The season has now changed from
Fall to winter with many snowflakes
Being sent from Heaven
In the month of December

It's time for all the children to
Believe in magic that there is a
Santa Claus I do agree

Opening their gifts on Christmas morn
This is the day that Jesus was born

This is the time of the season for sharing
Caring for everyone
And having a lot of fun

So many presents under the tree
Baby dolls that laugh and cry for little girls
And trucks for little boys
There are bicycles, trains and a scooter too
That bring so much happiness
And joy to you

Stockings are hung up on the fireplace
To be filled with many treats
This is so sweet

They are filled with fruits
Nuts, candy and a peppermint stick
Thanks to old St. Nick

Happiness

Is when you get thrills and
Chills all over your body from
Your head to your toes
It puts a smile on your face for
Everyone to see
This is the ways it's supposed to be

Your face glows in the morning light
Which makes you look so shining Bright

These feelings are passed along to
Others to make their day go as
smooth as one another

Please no more frowns upon your face
Only smiles are selected to fall upon
Your rosy cheeks for all to seek

A Chocolate Sundae

Yummy, yummy, yummy
You're so very delicious
To my tummy
There are layers and layers of frozen
Winter wonderland vanilla ice cream
I hope it's not very lumpy

You're dazzled with warm chocolate
Sauce upon this ice cream
It feels like velvet on your tongues
What a dream

It's topped with crunchy nuts
Lots and lots of whipped cream
With many different colors of
Sprinkles and a cherry on top

It's served in a small bowl with
A spoon for you to eat alone
Or with a special friend
Eat your hearts out
You will have a hard time stopping

A Sandbox

It's a beautiful day
Time to go out and play
In my sandbox

Gathering my pail and shovel
And cookie cutters looking
Forward to sitting on this gritty
Mound of sand
And hoping not get too much sand
In my hair
For Pete sake's I don't really care

I will have to get washed up from playing
In this grainy sand
So I will just have a lot of fun and
Witness that first hand

It's time for the day to end
Pick up my shovel and pail
And head to the house
Shaking off the sand that has
Covered me from my head
To my toes and all over

My clothes
Including my nose

Put my shovel and pail away
For another day when I can
Go out and play

Tasha, "My Yellow Lab Dog"

It's been a long time now since
I have seen you
You will always be in mommy's Heart
I loved you from the very start
And you loved me back
You were so very smart

You came to me at five month's old
With manners
This I was told

You have been the most loyal
And friendly dog ever
You will always be in mine
Heart forever

Love you Tasha Beam

Ice Skating

It's winter time and Jack Frost has
Just appeared
He froze over all the ponds, creeks
And lakes
For goodness sake

So now we can put on our ice skates
And glide across this clear frozen
Water of ice and snow
To grace and free motion
With a lot of emotion

Click, click with our sharp blades
On the bottom of our skates
We glide over this ice
With is pretty nice

Doing twirls, spins or doing a
Figure eight
All makes you feel pretty great

Don't skate too fast you might fall
On your ass

This wouldn't be a blast
You can skate alone or with
Your lover

My Transistor Radio

I received you as a
Christmas gift in 1950
I remember all so well that your
Brand was called Jewel

You are so amazing and cool
I was even lucky enough to
Take you to school

You lit up my life with all your
Sparkles that covered your dial
I walked around my neighborhood
With you for a mile
You brought me many smiles

You played awesome music
Soothing to my ear
Paul Anka "Put your Head on my Shoulders"

This song was my very favorite
I listened to this music for many years

You are gone now and you're so tired out

You must go and rest
You were once filled with a lot of zest

I will always remember this little radio
That gave me many years of memories

A Lighthouse

You are there for all of is to see
A quiet entity on the edge of a
Rugged cliff you are so tall and stiff

The breeze of the wind at night
Cast shadows upon you
That are so very scary

You look so alone at night under
The dark guiding lights
Oh my what a sight

Your light at the top of you
Shines so shining bright
Over the shadows of the dark ribbing
Waters of the sea at night

In the morning light you look so
Peaceful, calm and serene
So much magic to be seen

My Favorite Cat, "Whiskers"

I saw your picture in a book at the
Vets office on this sunny day in June

You needed a home and I needed
Someone to love
Once I saw you I knew that you
Would be mine

Even though you looked something like a raccoon
I took you home
You were so big and cute
With long whiskers
You were very special to me
I knew that whiskers would be your new name
Very soon

I will always remember how you followed
Me around
You were so heavy that your tummy
When walking was always on the ground

When watching TV you would snuggle
And cuddle up to me and put

Your paw on my heart
You were so very smart

There was so much love
Between me and you
This is so true

My Shirley Temple Doll

You sit upon my desk
In your beautiful pink
Taffeta dress

I am in awe with your
Beauty
You take away all my stress
Your mohair locks have never
Been touched
You are still like the day that
That you were born in 1930

You still have your original oil
Cloth shoes of ivory
A tag marked with your name
Shirley Temple still on the dress
And a straw bonnet to match
You are so surely blessed

You make me smile when I Am down
You were an awesome snatch

You are in such perfect condition

And I am so happy to be the one to Own you
Your head, arms and legs are made
Out of composition

I have loved you for many years and
Many more to come

My White Tail Deer

You come in the morning Light
Looking for food but
None is to be found
You knock on my window
To let me know
What you are looking for
Corn and seed that I
Usually put on the ground

I get your food and take it
To the place you like best
As I get close you take a very
Small gentle step backwards
So I can't touch you
I think this is a test

You look at me with those
Big gorgeous brown eyes
You are peaceful, gentle and fine

You run and jump so high that all I
Can see is your beautiful white tail
What a beautiful sight

A Pansy

You bring loving thoughts
For all of us to see
You are so mesmerizing and
Beautiful to our eyes
For me and you
Your sweet aroma of your
Petals are so breathtaking
You are not a surprise

You come in many different
Shapes and size
You lift up your smiling
Faces to the rays of the
Sunshine in the sky
That helps you grow so
Sassy and wise

You come in different colors
Like yellow, orange, purple
Violet, red, white, and blue
This is so true

When we look upon your smiling face
You make us feel so happy
It fills our hearts with a lot of love
Given from Heaven above

A Goldfinch

You perch your feathers upon
My Rose of Sharon Tree
Smelling the beautiful fragrance
That this tree makes for all to be
You eat seeds from my bird feeder
This couldn't get much sweeter

You flutter your yellow and black wings
All around and being so very proud
Flying next to my plants and trees

You have the company of all
The hummingbirds and the bees
There is so much magic I can see

You land on my burning bush
And you taste the sweet juice
Of each and every flower
Being so very careful not to
Get pushed

Then you fly away to
Return on another day

You even come on a day when
There is a rain shower

My First Kiss

A long time ago a young man walked into
My life, touched my hands and made my
Heart flutter

Then he whispered sweet nothings in my ear
And kissed me with lips as soft as butter

He has the most gorgeous smile is a very
Understanding loving young man

He has the most scrumptious hazel eyes
That just sparkled and twinkled

It's been many years since that day
And I would give anything just to be able
To steal one more kiss

Oh how I still remember

A Frog

Sitting upon your lily pad
In the light of the night
With misty dews from the
Cool and peaceful air
You sing so magically
Under the beautiful
Starry sky at night

You make so much heartfelt
Music for all to hear
You jump from one lily pad
To another singing and hoping
That your soul mate is near

Finding that special someone
This night to Love
That you will be so proud of

When they are found there will be
Two of you then
Sitting on the lily pad
Making beautiful music for all to hear
This is a definite wow

A Bakery

Sweet aroma from a bakery in
The early morning light
Gives you a warming embrace
With all its might

Glass cases are filled
With so many different choices
Oh so many that it's so hard
To decide
Maybe a donut that is plain and fried

There are jelly donuts that gleam with a
Confectionary icing on top
Sweet tasting cinnamon rolls with
The awesome smells of cinnamon
Throughout the shop

I need to pick one
I will choose a donut with many sprinkles
Being so careful not to get sprinkles in my hair

This couldn't get much sweeter
I do declare

I Promise

Hold my hand and walk with me
Through the green forest and around
The dark blue sea

I promise to Love you and show
You to the whole world for all
To see
I promise to be there in troubled times
All you have to do is hold my hand
And then you will hear the church
Bells chime

Hold my hand and walk with me under the
Beautiful blue sky
Hold me so tight and don't ever
Ask why

Hold my hand my Love and squeeze me so
Very tight and
Kiss me with your lips as soft as butter
Which will make my
Heart flutter

Hold my hand and promise you will
Always be there for me
And I will always
Be there for you

I Promise

The Freshman Dance

Going with a loving young man
To my first formal dance
Hoping for a little romance
Like a kiss on my cheek
This I will seek

Pretty up in a gorgeous pink
Taffeta ballerina gown
Stepping out into the night
Light with ballet slippers to
Match
I wore in my long brown hair a
Sparkling crystal crown
Feeling so grown up but I am
Only sixteen
But I felt like a Queen

I with a fella I had just met
At first sight he kissed me on
My cheek
What a surprise
Then I felt so weak

He took me into his arms and
Twirled me around to the beat of
The music
I being so very careful not to
Step on his feet

He took my hand and walked
Me home
And he finally kissed me on
My lips
He will always be my friend

A Glowing Candle

A lighted candle sheds
Its light throughout
The house
Being so quiet as a mouse

The burning light of a candle
Is nature's night light when It's dark
You need to be so careful not to
Have it drip it could leave a mark

A candle cast shadows into the
Dark room at night
What shapes it casts upon us is
What we think the shadows
Remind us of

Candles glow on the table when
You're alone or with your honey
Having a quiet evening and a
Romantic dinner
This couldn't get much sweeter

A Flowing Creek

Winter time has come to an end
Ice chucks still appear
Hoping that they will soon
Disappear

They are flowing with speedy
Delight
In the morning light
In the freezing waters
Of this amazing little creek
With all their might

It flows with soothing sounds
That are so relaxing and peaceful
To our minds
This will surely make you unwind

The beauty of your nature along
The creek banks are so
Breathtaking to our eyes
The deer take a sip of your
Water in the morning light
And gracefully run away

Not a surprise

Little children gather around the
Little creek hoping to catch a fish
Or two
When caught it will put a smile on
Their little faces
Now it's time to scurry and hurry
Back home
In hopes to have that fish for dinner
And please don't hurry

My Favorite Season "Fall"

It's a beautiful time of the year to see leaves
Turning different colors of yellow, orange and red
Admiring these leaves as they fall from above
And land on our heads

The colors of the leaves are so magnificent
To our eyes
They fall down on a breezy day from
Strong winds on trees that
God had made from Heaven above
Exquisite and bright and
Fall with all their might

They fall down in many different directions and
Cover the ground
We walk among them and hear crunch, crunch
Under our feet
What a beautiful sound

A Poem from the Soul

Abuse

What is abuse
I sure you it's not a
Warm and fuzzy feeling
It's a feeling that hurts your mind
And crushes your soul
All you want to do is run and hide
And hope and pray that these feeling
Will subside

I lived in abuse for thirty-two years and
Never told a soul
My communications from him was scribble
Words upon a yellow notebook paper
Placed on a table and then they
Would fall on the floor
Sometimes I would find them taped
To the kitchen door

I am no longer going through this abuse
I found courage and strength to go and tell
And found that I had resources to set me free
I can finally get out of this hell

I filed for Divorce and life couldn't get
Much sweeter
For all that I had gone through

"I am no longer a Victim"
"I am a Survivor"

Other Books by Karen

Shakespeare's Amazing Traveling Adventure
I am the project Manager

Be Positive, No Matter What,
My Journey Through Breast Cancer
Book One

Be Positive, No Matter what
Miracles Do Happen
Book Two

It's in the Bag My New Experiences
After Having Breast Cancer
Book Three

My Poems of Memories
From Childhood to Now
Book Four

At the end of our journey there is
hope for all of us.

Karen J. Nolan

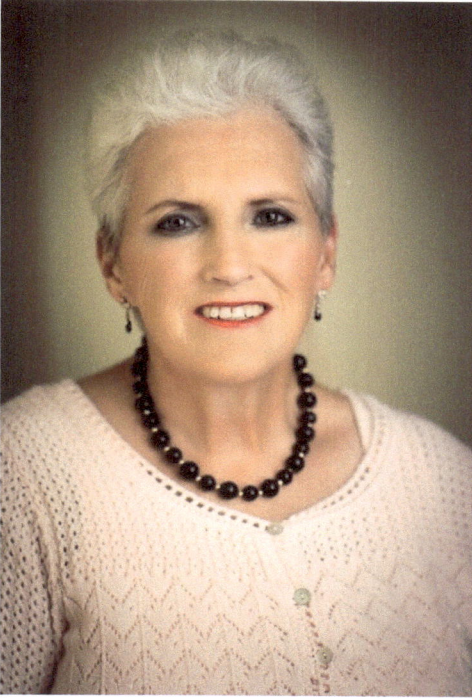

Karen Nolan is a mother of two children; she was a home child care provider for 29 years and a teacher's assistant at St. Louis school in Pittsford.

While raising her grandson Erick, she was involved with PET PRIDE and always had a new guest dog, or cat that sometimes became a member of the family.

Karen is living a joyful life full of blessings in Fairport, NY with 1 cat, and 2 dogs.

For group or educational copies email author.
Ask for our multiple discounts.
If you would like to talk to Karen J. Nolan or invite her to speak to your group or organization.

www.BePositiveNoMatterWhat.com

Distributed by Baker and Taylor, Ingram.
Everywhere Books Are Sold.

www.ingramcontent.com/pod-product-compliance
Lightning Source LLC
Chambersburg PA
CBHW042128080426
42735CB00001B/7